Jonathan Locke

Coding
On Software Design Process

ISBN: 978-0-615-40482-0

Cover design and photography by Nathania tenWolde.

Table of Contents

Introduction

About this Book

Description

In this book, industry veteran and Apache open source author, Jonathan Locke, discusses what he has learned over the years about the process of coding. He relates new ideas and methods that you can use to discover and refine your own best coding process.

Why This Book?

I started writing this book for the same reason that I originally started writing the web framework that was later named "Apache Wicket": I had a serious itch to scratch. The itch this time was this: I have found myself in recent years increasingly engaged in conversations with people about software development process. These have often been very interesting and exciting conversations and I've learned a lot from them. But the trouble with verbal conversations is that they have to end. There's never enough time. So, I wanted a place to put down some of the most interesting thoughts and discoveries I've had over the years where other people could pick them up and (hopefully) benefit from them at their leisure. I feel this book is very much a conversation starter, so if you have comments I'd be interested in hearing from you. My contact information is below.

About the Author

Jonathan is a chief architect, magazine columnist, author, speaker, mentor and practicing code artist. He is also the creator of Apache Wicket and a former member of the Java team at Sun Microsystems as well as the Microsoft Windows team. He resides in Seattle, Washington where he also pursues acting, directing, writing and producing theater (and maybe someday film). He is a proud member of the board at the phenomenal non-profit theater arts organization *Freehold*. He enjoys talking Seattle area software professionals into taking classes there and then smiles when they tell him it changed their lives.

jonathan.locke@gmail.com

About the Cover Artist

Nathania is a jack-of-all-trades artist living in Seattle. She is paid for her photography and oil painting, but also parades around as an actor, writer and mixed media artist. She aspires to create spaces, stories and objects that resonate with beauty, and has been known to pursue that end as far as organizing her library of 1000+ books by the colors of their spines.

nathania.tenwolde@gmail.com
reddressredress.blogspot.com

Acknowledgements

Thanks to Tim Boudreau for providing detailed and insightful comments on the first draft of this book. Thanks also to Eric Godwin for his thoughts as well as Cemal Bayramoglu of jWeekend (which specializes in best-practices software development and mentoring, including courses on Apache Wicket). And of course, a very special thanks to the core committers and members of the Apache Wicket community for being a great family to my open source baby.

Chapter 1

Practicing the Art

"In the beginner's mind there are many possibilities,
in the expert's there are few." — *Shunryu Suzuki*

This book is about practicing the art of coding.

The practice of writing artful code can be fun, inspiring and rewarding. Unfortunately, your pointy haired boss, and even you yourself, may tend to think of artful code as being impractical; as something that has little to do with your day job. *Nothing could be further from the truth.* In fact, engaging in a day-to-day practice of coding as an art form is not only a supremely practical matter, it is also *essential to both personal and organizational success.*

The vast majority of software books out there are, at some level, vocational cookbooks. They demonstrate how to achieve some specific desired result through a series of steps. While these books may be a practical way to learn some specific skill, they are a bit like junk food in their effect on your developing craft — at best they suggest quick fixes that solve today's problems and at worst reading them is a distraction which actually slows your progress as an aspiring code artist. To learn solely through practical experience and by reading such cookbooks is *necessarily* a long and painful trek (been there, done that). If you want instead to advance quickly in your art, you need to study and improve *process* not result. To the master artisan, *what* is accomplished is not nearly so important as *how it is accomplished.* Unlike all those result-focused cookbooks, this book aims to show you *how* to code. Or rather, how to teach yourself how to code, by observing and refining your own process.

People and organizations who focus on results (code) and not process (coding) are *by definition* blind to the myriad of opportunities that arise to refine their process. Since they are not *actually paying attention* to what they are doing, they have very limited ability to improve. Instead they buy stacks of cookbooks, experiment with management methodologies and attempt to measure their (unavoidably lackluster) results.

On the opposite hand, people and organizations who are aware of *process* and who make a conscious, focused effort to refine their process will find that they are able to improve their day-to-day craft. As a result these people move forward in terms of their results, often dramatically when measured over a long period of time. But the relatively impressive results they produce (which management will almost certainly still dwell on, unfortunately) are actually just a by-product of their improved process. This is true in every art form and it is equally true in coding.

In roughly thirty years of pursuing coding as an art form, I have spent a lot of time thinking about and refining my own process and discovered that the more *deliberately* and *precisely* I do this, the more it accelerates my growth. This book is an attempt to set down and share my own process discoveries and observations so that they might benefit other aspiring code artists.

In reading this book, please keep in mind that even if I do have a lot of very strong opinions about what makes good coding process (and this is hopefully one of the reasons you are reading this book), in the end there is no *best way* to code that applies to everyone. Each person's process is uniquely theirs and I am simply sharing how I have learned to code, how I think about coding and what works best for me. In the spirit of open investigation, you should try on my ideas for size and then take whichever ones fit and throw out the rest.

Enjoy!

Chapter 2

Creating a Foundation

"Must be present to win." — Modern Buddhist saying

Must be present to win. This is at least as true in coding as it is in any other pursuit. The more aware you are of your process, the more opportunity you have to consciously shape it. The less self-aware you are, the more likely you are to fall into bad habits. Developing awareness is not easy in a world full of demands and distractions, but one tried-and-true place to start is in your own body.

Being Present

Since coding is an intellectual exercise at heart, we unfortunately tend to forget our bodies. However, paying close attention to your body's particular needs and rhythms can be at least as important as improving your intellectual process or your technical education. The basics are required: good sleep and quality time away from work, plenty of water, healthy foods, appropriate medical care and regular breaks throughout the day for breathing, laughing, socializing, stretching, walking and exercise. Without a solid physical foundation to work from, your intellectual abilities will weaken and your mental and physical health may even decline.

I find that a couple short walks each day as well as a quick bit of yoga or weight lifting and a small glass of water every 20 to 30 minutes is enough to keep my body and mind fully focused. Since it's hard to remember to do this when I'm coding, I find a break timer to be invaluable. A break timer is a software program that pops up periodically and reminds you to take breaks. I use an application called

"Time Out" on my MacBook (http://www.dejal.com/timeout/), which allows you to schedule both "micro-breaks" and longer breaks over the course of your day. Remembering to take breaks is a crucial habit and worth working on. If you're rushed, even just standing up and stretching for 60 seconds is better than plowing through.

It's always surprising to me how much better I code when my body is really consciously being taken care of as I work. And of course, when I neglect my body I quickly get physically and mentally stressed. This usually happens more around project deadlines, although I am slowly getting better and better at fighting this tendency. And of course, getting stressed only causes me to make more mistakes, which feeds back to cause even more stress and so on. Worst of all, deadline pressure tends to make me less self-aware, which makes it all that much harder to handle. For me, the key to staying conscious of my process is really taking my break timer seriously. When I do that, everything else falls into place because it brings my mind back to awareness.

> *Take regular breaks using a break timer to maintain your*
> *physical health and improve your process awareness.*

In general, my advice when you get stressed out by a project deadline is this: *slow down to hurry up.* Trust your process enough to step back and take care of yourself as you would without a deadline and the work will be far, far more likely to get done well and done on schedule. Holding your nose to the grindstone and trying to stay in a coding "zone" that doesn't truly exist because you are abusing your body is a great way to not only hurt yourself physically and emotionally, but also increase your odds of missing your deadline. If you push hard and mindlessly enough, you can even cause a lot of structural damage to your project that will take time out of future milestones to correct, increasing your negative feedback loop even more down the road.

I know all this as first-hand truth because I've worked both ways and seen other people working both ways. "Slow down to hurry up" is good advice for the simple reason that it observably works. Not only is it less stressful to be good to yourself, it is also better for your near-term schedule, your long-term schedule and your project's future in general. In practice, this policy of consciously slowing down and working very carefully and deliberately as deadlines approach has had a very big practical pay-off for me, personally: most projects I've led in recent years have come in on or slightly ahead of schedule, even when they seemed to be running behind a bit near the end. My managers generally love me now and give me tremendous freedom as a result, which makes my projects even less stressful. My old negative feedback loop has turned into a positive one.

> *Don't rush when things get stressful. Slow down to hurry up.*

There is a lot more to say about the art of scheduling and executing a project, but working on your physical process will give you a strong head start. In fact, this section is first because it is truly fundamental. *Without a strong and reliable physical foundation, you cannot have a strong coding process.* It will take time and effort to build this foundation, so I suggest you start by simply making a habit of observing yourself at work and making small incremental changes. It will take a considerable amount of time to refine your physical process to the point where it is strong and reliable, but it is definitely well worth the effort.

Feeling

Your feelings and personal inclinations also play a very critical role in your work process. It is important to observe yourself and how you change over time — throughout the hours of the day and the days of the week, but also through project cycles, months, seasons and years. What it is that excites you? What distracts you? What turns you off? What wears you out? When do you like to work with others? When do you need time alone to focus? Who do you work best with? What challenges you? What bores you? What makes you feel confident? Inadequate? How well do you communicate your needs to others? Is the organization you're working for meeting your needs? What do you do when your needs aren't being met? Are you fulfilling an important role? Is your company doing something that matters to you? What makes you happy? Angry? Worried? Stressed? Pessimistic? Positive? What makes you laugh? What makes you feel valued? What feels most like fun?

Next consider this: what improvements or shifts can you make based on these observations? And are there other people in your group that can help you to make these shifts to a better way of working? A full and conscious exploration of your emotional self and your social relationships at work is a prerequisite to refining your process and finding your stride. Really working on this is no small undertaking for anyone, but the rewards can be enormous and just being steadily aware of this part of your job can be a huge step forward, particularly if you feel stuck or unhappy.

> *Refine your process, and don't be afraid to ask others for help doing it.*

For myself, I have learned over the years that I tend to take on more responsibilities than I probably should and that I don't spend nearly enough time communicating what it is that I need from other people that I work with. As I have improved at working with others, I have found much to my surprise that some of the tasks that bore me are exciting or interesting to others. On the opposite hand, some of the things that I find the most frustrating and difficult are tasks that my coworkers don't mind doing nearly as much. For example, understanding all the intricacies of configuring Linux or dealing with Maven project files is something that one of my coworkers has really very little trouble with, while I really excel at developing novel software designs that push the envelope. I was surprised to discover that this sort of work that I find very comfortable and interesting, is actually extremely uncomfortable, stressful and even scary to the same coworker. By communicating with each other about this, we've been able to split up our work much more effectively and we are both happier for it.

<hr>

*Have regular, honest discussions with coworkers
on individual and group coding processes.*

<hr>

Another important learning for me relates to how I feel when feature changes and problems show up, particularly under deadline pressure. A very unhelpful habit that I've had to break is my tendency to want to address issues and make everything better right away. This tends to make me feel stressed out and like I'm falling behind. But in fact, how quickly and perfectly these issues get resolved has turned out not to be the major issue after all. At least in the group I'm working with right now, the most important thing to people who are giving me this kind of feedback is for them to feel that the issue has been heard and understood (asking appropriate clarifying questions is actually a very good way to let people know that you've really heard them) and that a priority has been set for it. Once this has been done, actually resolving the issue simply becomes part of our team process over time, rather than sitting squarely on my shoulders. In this light, it is very critical to my process (and to others on our team) to make good and appropriate use of our bug database and to communicate this need to stakeholders in my projects. People are actually very understanding about the fact that I am a limited resource and they are willing to help organize my work so that I am more effective in achieving our group goals.

Another emotional difficulty for me can be the feelings that "drudge work" can bring up for me. There are times when my emotional state is more ready for this sort of work and times when it is less so. For example, I find that I am very ready for the hardest problems and the most intricate work early in the morning, and that by afternoon I am much more willing to do rote tasks that would have annoyed me to no end in the morning. By organizing my tasks so that the fun work is mostly done when I most need things to be fun, in the morning, and the drudgery is mostly put off into the afternoon, I have been able to make some peace with the inevitable make–work tasks that come up in the course of a project.

It may take some time to sort through your own process in this way, and you may find that you need to revisit your process when your coworkers change or you take on a new project. As with developing awareness of your body at work, developing awareness of your work feelings and your work relationships is also something that needs to be done continuously. I recommend developing a habit of checking in with your feelings as well as your body each time your break timer goes off. Just ask yourself the question "how are things going?" The results you can get just by following this simple process may be quite surprising and rewarding. And when you find yourself stressing out and ignoring your break timer, ask yourself "why am I not trusting my process?" The answers to these questions can be quite interesting and at times surprising, and checking in with yourself like this and possibly communicating with others about your findings can help put things back on track.

Thinking

Just as greater awareness of your physical and emotional process can help to make your job more rewarding and more fun, greater awareness of your thought processes can help you to refine the intellectual part of your practice and make you a stronger problem solver. It's important in approaching this to remember that everyone is different. Pay attention to yourself as you work. What pace is comfortable to you? What sort of problems do you like? Loathe? What do you find uncomfortable to think about? What problems excite you? What time of day are you most ready to tackle hard problems? Do you need time to digest certain types of problems? What happens to you when you are interrupted? Are you able to put work down easily? How easily can you get back into it? At what point do you become fatigued? How many hours is your ideal work day? Is Friday as easy for you as Monday? At what point do your efforts become error-prone? Do you reach a point where you consistently start making mistakes? Is there a way you can organize your work to take advantage of these observations?

I am of the strong belief that the vast majority of software designers and programmers and the companies that they work for work *far too many hours*. These companies and often the individuals within them create a very simplistic mythology that the only way to get more done is through "hard work", not meaning focused work, but rather putting in long hours. In reality, software is a finesse game with problems that don't yield easily to the brute force stoicism of simply staying at work longer (notice my word choice there: if you observe many of these "hard-working" people, you will find that the majority of these extra hours are spent doing non-work tasks or dealing with problems that wouldn't exist if they had been able to bring more focus to their work in the first place, which they can't because they are too overworked). For companies that are willing to experiment, working smarter and with better focus over fewer hours will definitely achieve far greater results for everyone involved. And the difference between the two approaches only increases over longer periods of time. I know this because I've been there and done that. The well-run, focused projects with shorter hours get easier and easier over time while the "hard-working" projects with long hours and poor focus inevitably get less agile and harder to maintain as the legacy of all those extra hours comes home to roost in the form of fatigue, bad design decisions, bad code and ultimately burnout and turnover.

My own ideal day is limited to four or five hours of focused, concentrated work and maybe one hour of "administrivia"; certainly nothing longer than six hours unless there's something really exceptional going on. Anything significant beyond this length invariably produces mental fatigue which in turn *always* creates cascading sequences of mistakes that I call "code churn" (large amounts of work that accomplish little or nothing because they don't really solve the problem at hand and ultimately result in a need to re-factor *again*). I know this from direct experience because I have worked five hour days in the past at more than one farsighted company (believe it or not, there are some out there!) and I've never been able to equal the long-term productivity I had at those companies when comparing them with companies where i worked eight hours a day. Furthermore, the jobs where I've worked more than eight hours a day have been the very lowest in terms of long-term productivity. By far. For me, it's this simple: I can work eight plus hours a day because the company I work for mandates it or in order to try to get something done on a deadline, but *there will be a price to pay* and that price for me is: fatigue, an increase in code churn, a decline in code quality, an increase in stress, a decrease in job satisfaction and eventually long-term burnout.

Although every programmer is different, I suspect that we are more alike in this regard than management at most companies is willing to consider. The benefit to companies that are willing to give this some thought is a potentially significant competitive advantage. Consider this: after a full year of working five hour days at one particularly wonderful startup, I was ready to *enjoy* a vacation, but for the first time in my software career, I didn't *need* one. The difference there is *enormous*: I was not only more productive at that job than any other, but after a year of hard, prolific product development I was actually hungry for more, rather than thinking about how much longer I could stick with my job before needing a significant break (either through unpaid time, a hiatus or a job change) to recover.

> *Learn what your focusing limits are and respect them as much as possible.*

Besides overwork, the next most difficult issue that I have to deal with on a regular basis is interruption. When I am "in the zone" and coding something complex or novel, probably the worst thing possible is a sudden interruption. I have spent some time observing what happens to me when I'm interrupted and it's bad enough that I've come up with a number of improvements in my process and the process in my group which help a great deal.

The first is that I have worked out with my coworkers a rough daily schedule for heads-down designing and coding. I typically do all of my most difficult problem solving between 6:30 AM and about 10 AM. And after that much heavy concentration, I'm much less useful at that sort of work for the rest of the day. During those early hours, many of my coworkers are not around to interrupt me, but the ones who are have some awareness that I'm likely trying to concentrate. After my focus time is over, I try to shift my thought processes to more group-oriented activities and make myself very available to interruption and interaction as other people on my team often want my advice on specific problems that they are trying to solve.

Besides knowing when each of us is working in a focused way, we also have an informal protocol that we try to use when it is necessary to interrupt each other. I work remotely, which pretty much eliminates the problem of someone walking into my office. My co-workers and I instead use e-mail and Skype to communicate by instant message and voice. There is something much more immediate and distracting about a voice call (or an office visit) as an interruption than there is about an instant message. Even less immediate is an e-mail. And even less immediate than that is putting a request in our bug database.

Our protocol is simply to try to pick a good time to interrupt each other and try to pick the minimum level of distraction that will resolve our issue. In addition, when we have a relatively high priority issue, we always check Skype's do-not-disturb status before instant messaging each other to ask first if a voice call would be okay. All this said, some interruptions are simply unavoidable and we're all aware of that. If a production system goes down and our clients are unhappy, an interruption is a good thing. Fortunately, there are very, very few such interruptions in my group.

> *Discuss interruptions within your group and agree on best practices*
> *to minimize their impact on those who are sensitive to them.*

It can be really healthy for group dynamics to discuss these sort of issues regularly. Just talking about our concentration needs and work habits as a group, for example, has led to enormous reductions in everyone's stress levels and has further helped us to communicate about pressing issues more effectively as well. It may take some additional work if you have an office door and a pointy-haired boss that loves to stop by and change your game plan completely every fifteen minutes, but it is communication work with a big payoff: a low stress, highly effective workplace where everyone has a lot more fun.

> *Discuss issues regularly with your group and keep refining your group's processes.*

Chapter 3

Practicing in Reality

"In theory there is no difference between theory and practice. In practice there is." — *Yogi Berra*

The difference between what is taught in college and graduate school and what is practiced in the software industry is, unfortunately, enormous. Well-meaning academics expound high-brow theories of software development and demonstrate best coding practices in neat, highly mathematical (and often unreadable) examples, but never apply their methods to large or practical projects. Overworked coders who once heard all this stuff in graduate school proceed to give up on these best practices as being unrealistic "ivory tower" stuff that they don't have time for. "Sounds good, but I have to ship a product." In reality, both sides could learn a thing or two.

Incrementalism

In approaching the thorny issue of how to refine your practice of software art under what are essentially factory conditions in the software industry, it's important to keep perspective. You won't be able to turn a typical project into an idealized model of OO design in short order. But hey, Rome wasn't built in a day. In fact, if someone had suggested "Let's build Rome!" it seems more than likely that this person's urban development project would have gone unfunded and we'd be short one of the world's great cities.

The question usually seems to come down to this: How can you get started towards a better practice when it never seems like a good time to start? There's always a fire-drill or a deadline at some companies and the effect can be, frankly, demoralizing. But while green-fields development has it's place, the truth is that you don't necessarily need to stop the world or start a new project from the ground up to improve your coding process. You can break down complex problems and solve them one step at a time and similarly refine your coding process itself in small increments. In fact, although investment in any art form requires *some* change and some level of commitment to the future (and the more the better, to a point), I would argue that it is only very rarely desirable to stop the world and start over.

So, while you may have a product to ship and that product may have its warts, I doubt this really excludes the possibility that you might refine your art. In fact, if you have the will to do it, you can refine your process and pursue your art even under very adverse conditions. Even at your miserable day job. Even buried under ten levels of pointy-haired bosses on some horrific J2EE project. That project may not be an ideal circumstance if you foolishly aspire to perfection, but if it is true that "smart people learn from their mistakes while truly clever people learn from the mistakes of others", isn't your day-job actually an ideal learning environment? Maybe all you have to do is shift your thinking. Instead of focusing on the result (which is extremely bad at most software companies), you can focus on the process instead, which can evolve in a satisfactory way. The most powerful way to approach this is to work on your thinking habits while you attempt to build and expand out "pockets of competence" in your product.

Prefer the incremental building and expansion of "pockets of competence".
Avoid stopping the world to rewrite (when possible).

Questioning

Thinking is like exercise. You get stronger by doing a lot of it and it can be painful to get started again when you've stopped doing it for a while. While undoubtedly you have tough project deadlines and cut and dried solutions that will get you there, the oh-so-typical repetition of what worked last time can be effective, but it can also be a convenient excuse to avoid engaging in a kind of work that people in all walks of life will go to almost any length to avoid: *actually thinking*. By thinking, I don't mean seeming thoughtful or intelligent. I don't mean quoting other people or understanding thick books. I don't mean repeating or rephrasing something you already know. I don't mean demonstrating hard-won expertise. *True thinking is always an exploration of the unknown*, and as such it necessarily comes with a certain amount of risk and discomfort.

I find that the best kind of thought comes from asking questions rather than trying to find answers. In fact, the more naive or simple the question is, the more interesting the ideas it typically leads to. This is one reason that I love to work with beginners. They ask questions that I have, after thirty years, learned not to ask. Education and practical experience both produce a certain kind of narrowness of thinking, while beginners still have a very wide scope of imagination. As Shunryu Suzuki said in the quote in the front of this book "In the beginner's mind there are many possibilities, in the expert's there are few."

> *Strongly prefer questions to answers.*
> *Stay flexible in your thinking.*

You can apply this "beginner's mind" approach to your own work. If you make a habit of questioning what you do, this will naturally create a certain quality of self-awareness in your work. And this self-awareness will automatically lead to new ideas for process refinements. Although you may not be able to undo the hundreds of thousands of lines of badly written code on your current project, you *can* take process refinement ideas and execute on them immediately. And the results you can get from even small process refinements can be very immediate and gratifying. What's more, the more you do this kind of work the easier it gets (as the mind is a muscle) and the net effect of discovering hundreds of new process improvements over years becomes enormous. Best of all, an incremental practice of self-aware process refinement is possible even under the most adverse industrial software conditions.

Thinking Small

To practice your art in a realistic, day-to-day software development context, what you want to do to move forward is think small. *Really small.* Rather than looking at the large-scale structure of your project (and if it's a typical software industry project, it probably has little if any object-oriented architecture to it at all), you should focus on the small. The biggest opportunities for process gains and also for moving your project forward will be in applying a portion of your thought (as much as possible) to what I call "micro-architecture".

A micro-architecture is the design of something, no larger than a package, consisting of only a few simple, co-operating objects and interfaces. It can be as small as a single object or even an interface with a single method. A micro-architecture is a small pocket of design focus and competence that serves as a seed for larger architectures and for the expansion of competence. It is an incredibly clear, elegant abstraction that isolates a problem and solves it in a highly general way. The best such designs crystalize a concept so clearly and simply that the vision never needs to be revised.

Micro-architectures serve as synergistic building blocks. The accumulation of solid, trustworthy, flexible micro-architectures creates a foundation of *atoms* out of which you can build molecules, compounds and materials as you expand pockets of competence outwards to the macro level where they ultimately have the potential to organically structure your entire project and even your company's software in general.

I will explain more about how to create solid micro-architectures in chapter five, but the basic idea is to divide a problem down until it won't divide any further. When you have successfully narrowed your problem space to the level of an atomic idea, you will have created an abstraction with real leverage, focus and generality.

To give some form to this rather abstract discussion, let's look at "conversion" as an example problem that has been solved countless times and rarely, if ever, to the satisfaction of all. The reason that most of these solutions are unsatisfying is that in every solution I've seen, a truly atomic micro-architecture was never reached. Too many questions were left open because the problem space wasn't divided to an atomic level. This failure to define a solid micro-architecture then creates all kinds of "code churn" because it necessitates the creation of still more conversion frameworks with different feature sets in the future. Why? Nobody ever sat with the problem long enough to clearly define what it means to convert in the abstract. And if this sounds like philosophy, in some sense it is.

To make our example even more concrete, suppose you are developing a REST application that does a lot of conversion to and from String objects. This is a pretty common problem and the naive design for your converter framework might be:

```
public interface StringConverter<Type>
{
   String toString(Type object);
   Type toObject(String string);
}
```

Unfortunately, this would-be micro-architecture isn't really atomic to begin with. But to make matters worse, a co-worker will probably decide to expand the interface when they recognize that there is a problem with localization:

```java
public interface StringConverter<Type>
{
  String toString(Type object, Locale locale);
  Type toObject(String string, Locale locale);
}
```

But the "improvement" of adding this parameter is actually a step backwards. The design is now headed in a sadly all-to-typical direction: growing classes, expanding parameter lists and ultimately interoperability problems. The problem is becoming less focused, less atomic and less reusable. It is also getting harder to understand. To really crystalize our micro-architecture, we need to step back from this kind of thinking and take another approach.

Suppose we instead ask the question "What is conversion, really?" And by this, I mean "What is the simplest form of the problem of conversion in general?" If we consider this for a moment, we are likely to come up with a far more general and powerful definition of conversion. In fact, the interface below represents any type conversion in Java whatsoever:

```java
public interface Converter<From, To>
{
  To convert(From from);
}
```

It's very hard to argue with this interface because it defines what it means to convert in Java. Even a converter that turns image streams into images could be expressed like this:

```
Converter<InputStream, BufferedImage>
```

Since we really can't boil conversion down any further we will define this simplest interface as an atomic micro-architecture that we can then use to build a StringConverter "molecule":

```
public interface StringConverter<Type>
{
  Converter<Type, String> toStringConverter();
  Converter<String, Type> toObjectConverter();
}
```

In fact, there are at least a couple of issues that are not handled here. One is localization, as we noted earlier. Another is location of the most appropriate converter when several conversions are possible. Another is that we may want some method for handling errors in the case of failed conversions. But I would argue that each of these are actually — you guessed it — other micro-architectures. And most importantly, none of these other dimensions of conversion will ever affect the Converter interface we've defined. That should stand the test of time and can be relied on into the distant future for interoperability between software units of all different sizes that need to convert objects from one form to another. By thinking small, we have taken a big step forward.

Scaling Thought

One of the advantages of thinking small in your architectures is that it will also help you to think bigger. A very typical problem of present-day software projects is that non-existent micro-architecture leads to simplistic and non-object-oriented thinking regarding larger units. If you haven't really thought about the atoms of your design or what sort of molecules you can build from them, why should you expect that the large-scale design for what you are building is going to work? Most modern software designs stop at the macro level of servers and modules, which is a bit like making a design for a skyscraper and then deciding to use whatever is handy for building materials at construction time. At the present time, freely available materials (with a few rare exceptions like the often cited Java collections package) might include the software equivalents of cardboard, plywood and duct tape. Sure, you will wind up with something that has the shape of a skyscraper, but it may not have the sort of characteristics your clients might expect from such a building!

If you instead invest in micro-architectural infrastructure and start building up a vocabulary for expressing larger designs, it can help to discover your macro-architecture. If you have a really great micro-architecture for messaging, for example, this may make it easier to think about component boundaries. If you have a micro-architecture for object-oriented logging (as opposed to trace logging, which is virtually useless by comparison), you can apply this across your servers to improve the richness and availability of runtime execution information. And so on.

Another place where micro-architectures can help is that they can serve to define a standard of manufacturing. If it's defined in a reusable micro-architecture how errors are reported across all other designs, it will be much easier to reuse those components. If your error micro-architecture is carefully designed to work with your logging architecture, you will gain further synergies. In fact, the same goes for all cross-cutting concerns in your domain: application configuration, component wiring, network access, parsing, validation, database access and so on. It's getting the nuts and bolts right that enables a high-quality, large-scale architecture to be discovered and implemented. If you instead start trying to build a skyscraper with available parts (and most freely available parts don't have very good design), you will ultimately create something that maybe looks like a skyscraper from a distance, but which doesn't function like one and cannot be easily extended or cost-effectively maintained.

If you instead invest time in thinking small, over time you will find that you are more and more able to build large, extensible, testable, reliable systems in less time. The simple reason for this is that if you do good micro-architectural design, the lion's share of your code is going to be reusable in the next project. To give you some idea of the ratios you should expect, my current projects are composed of about 50% fully reusable code, 30% reusable domain models with probably only about 20% product-specific glue. Once you have a solid, object-oriented base established to start new projects from, you can expect those projects to be far less work. But besides making better products faster, this sort of high quality work process is a lot more fun, which in turn means your company will attract more attention and better talent.

Prefer defining micro-architectural standards to increase code reuse and improve testability and interoperability.

Chapter 4

Writing

"Poor Faulkner. Does he really think big emotions come from big words? He thinks I don't know the ten-dollar words. I know them all right. But there are older and simpler and better words, and those are the ones I use. "

— Ernest Hemingway

Code as Language

Although mathematical abilities may apply to algorithmic programming, it is actually language skill that is at the heart of object-oriented programming. We may think of a class as being written in Java (and ultimately the compiler does interpret it that way), but it is actually a linguistic description of state and behavior in two languages simultaneously: the Java programming language and *the coder's native tongue.*

This is an important distinction that is sometimes lost on people who have strong math skills and relatively weak language and/or communications skills. When you write Java code, you are not really writing to be understood by the compiler, but to be understood by yourself and your fellow programmers in the future. In this light, code that executes perfectly and has all the intended effects is still not necessarily *good code.* For code to be well-written, it needs to be highly legible, even to relatively casual observers.

Since this is an English language book and Java's core classes are also written in English, I will be discussing English Java from this point forward, but the discussion itself should easily be applicable to

Dutch Java, French Java or Chinese Java. You might think, by the way, that non-native English speakers are at an inherent disadvantage, and while this does have some truth, non-native speakers that are highly motivated may actually have certain advantages because they have an outsider's perspective and because they may bother to look up words instead of assuming they know exactly what they mean. Which reminds me in passing of a funny conversation I had years ago with a Russian co-worker. He had been trying to quit smoking and so one day he asked me in his heavy Russian accent, "So, Jon. Can you tell me? Why are the turkeys cold?" Only a native English speaker such as myself could miss such an obvious puzzle.

> *Prefer intuitive, readable software. Create coding standards*
> *that enhance readability and follow them.*

Precision

To code well in Java, you must be as precise with the English language as possible. On the one hand, this means boiling names, concepts and statements down to their minimum as the Hemingway quote above suggests (or as Pascal suggested when he said "I would not have made this [letter] so long, but I did not have the leisure to make it shorter"). While on the opposite hand, never boiling things down so much that you lose precision. The English used in code must be extremely precise because the named concepts must be very specific in order for the design to be accurate.

Although terser, less readable code will still compile and execute identically, using the wrong words to describe your problem will inevitably lead to misconceptions, inaccurate abstractions and ultimately bad and buggy implementation that is hard to test. Conversely, you can often detect mistakes very early on by paying extraordinarily close attention to your word usage. When you are struggling with code, it is probably because you are laboring under some misconception or other. And if you have misconceived something it is nearly certain that you will find that it is because you have been using the wrong language to describe it.

While you do want to boil down your language so that it is intuitively understood, it must still be precise, which means using proper English and avoiding technical jargon and uncommon usage as much as possible. To this end, the very first rule of thumb you should adopt is to completely abolish the use of abbreviations in your code and to come to an agreement on any domain abbreviations that you will accept because they are *truly a better expression* of the idea at hand than the unabbreviated phrase. For example, URL is short for Uniform-ResourceLocator but URL is so commonly understood and used that the long spelling of the acronym is actually less recognizable.

Strongly prefer un-abbreviated language in all cases.
Maintain an agreed-upon list of exceptions.

If anything, I would recommend biasing yourself strongly towards names that are very precise, even if those names are a bit "too long" for some on your team. Not agreeing to spell things out is inviting trouble as abbreviations are a slippery slope that can make code arbitrarily difficult to read. If you are looking at a variable called "dir" by itself, how are you going to know if it is short for "direction" or "directory?" Does "inst" stand for "instance" or "instruction?" Does "db" mean "database" or "decibels?" Besides creating ambiguity, if you abbreviate you can create a need for accurate documentation and coder education that wouldn't otherwise exist. If you use the term "oid", for example, the majority of coders will probably know what you mean. If you instead use the term "objectIdentifier", even your pointy-haired boss or your summer intern will be able to guess. On my team, we are very rigorous about this and spell out even very commonly abbreviated words like "identifier", "index", "object", "application", "source", "destination" and so on. As much as possible, our code reads like ordinary English.

The risk to your project in cutting this particular corner is this: if you allow abbreviations in your code, it is *guaranteed* that everyone on your team will have a different idea of what is acceptable. For some, "dst" is a fine abbreviation for destination (although it could also mean distance). For others, "var2", "j", "arr2obj", or "swpx" will be just as acceptable. Over time, your codebase will become relatively illegible as it starts to decline to the level of your least legible coders. The simple truth is this: if you always use the full name for something, your intention can be understood. This has an enormous impact on design, implementation, testing, maintainability and future agility, as code written to this standard becomes inherently self-documenting.

In addition to ambiguity created by abbreviations, your code can suffer from other kinds of vagueness and ambiguity. A particular area of concern here is what happens to your names when you resort to using primitive types. If you use Java as an object-oriented language and create objects instead of using primitives, your variable names will be shorter and easier to read. Using primitive types, on the other hand, invites not only lack of safety and testability, but additionally, either ambiguity or longer variable names. For example, is "float distance" a value in meters or feet? And what if the documentation for that variable isn't kept up to date? While it's certainly clearer to name your variable "float distanceInMeters" if you really must use a primitive type, the best solution is to use the Java type system to create an object representing distance as a concept. By using a Java object, not only can you apply design patterns and unit testing and so forth, but declaration of your type will be obvious and unambiguous: "Distance distance." Or better yet, you can describe the intent of that distance instead of trying to encode the type in the name: "Distance toCornerStore." Now you're cooking with gas!

> *Prefer the use of types (classes and interfaces) to primitives.*
> *Consider omitting the class name (where it makes sense) from field*
> *names and local variable names. If you've declared something*
> *that's not a primitive, everyone already knows what type it is.*

Once you get used to creating readable, unambiguous names, the next step is to work on conceptual clarity. My method here is to keep working the name until I get the concept right. To do this, get and use a desktop thesaurus and make full use of your IDE's refactoring tools to fix and update names everywhere as your conceptions change. When you're coding away and you've suddenly got that feeling that you haven't quite nailed the name of something, *stop!* Instead of plowing ahead, switch to your thesaurus and think about what it is that you really mean. More often than not, when you finally find exactly the right word or words, the solution will suddenly get much easier to code.

The reason for this is quite simple: your brain is wired for language, and when you start expressing a solution in language that is even slightly incorrect, all your associations are also going to be slightly incorrect (if not *more* incorrect). Getting the right word or words figured out is the first step in creating a lasting solution to any problem. And, of course, it's when you start using imprecise language, placeholders or vague abstractions that you will go furthest astray. Beware in particular of really general words like "context", "object", "entry", "item" or "manager" (which are *almost always* crutches being used in place of accurate thinking)... unless that really is *exactly the most accurate concept.*

> *If you are having trouble naming something, stop and pay attention!*
> *Avoid trying to code what you can't name accurately.*

Grammar

Statements in well-written object-oriented code should read almost like English language sentences with backwards ordering, where (loosely speaking) objects are "nouns" and methods are "verbs." Extending this further, I like to think of object properties as "adjectives" and method parameters as "adverbs". *The legibility of your code depends not so much on comments, but on how well you have broken down the concepts involved into proper parts of speech out of which you can form self-explanatory sentences.*

To illustrate this point, many coders represent a duration of time as either a java.util.Date object (which actually represents a point in time (rather badly) and not a duration) or as a long value (which is an unsafe primitive value that can hold any integer value at all (including negative values) and depends on proper interpretation, which must be documented by hand and the documentation read and carefully obeyed).

These are both, almost needless to say, *really terrible choices* and should be avoided in favor of a Duration object of some sort (Apache Wicket and Joda Time both provide more appropriate objects or you can roll your own). This object should encapsulate the concept of a duration of time, and if you look up "duration" in a dictionary, it is indeed a noun. When you add appropriate verbs that operate on this noun, it becomes possible to compose highly self-explanatory statements about durations of time.

For example, if you want your Java code to pause for an hour and half, instead of writing this unfortunately familiar chunk of code:

```
try
{
  Thread.sleep(90 * 60 * 60 * 1000);
}
catch (InterruptedException e)
{
}
```

you can instead write something with the Wicket Duration class that reads almost exactly like English:

```
Duration.hours(1.5).sleep();
```

Which really only needs a comment if there is a need to explain *why* the code is sleeping, because even a non-programmer can probably tell you what it does.

But the story just gets better when you build out your domain and add other concepts that co-operate with this Duration class. Let's look at Wicket's Time class, for example. Suppose that you wanted to find out how long a piece of code takes to execute. You already know what this looks like with long values and System.currentTimeMillis (ugh, abbreviations and primitive types again!). Here's what it looks like with well-defined Time and Duration concepts instead:

```
Time start = Time.now();

[...]

Duration elapsed = start.elapsedSince();
```

Okay, so this is all good and well, but you may be thinking that this is a toy example; that things get trickier when you start coding more complicated objects. But that is not actually the case if you are doing it right. In my experience, the opposite is true. If your objects are getting tricky and complex (and typically buggy), it is probably because at some level you have blurred your concepts and that usually occurs because you are using bad grammar, either because you have conflated parts of speech or because you have created some new, ungrammatical word.

For example, a very common problem is that people create funny compound nouns, which are objects that represent two or more noun concepts at the same time. For example, a DogVolcano or a LobsterMuffin. Unfortunately, when you created your DogVolcano you probably never noticed how badly mixed the concept was because you never stopped to think about the meaning of that name. You were in a rush to get something coded (who isn't) and so you called it something vague but professional sounding like "ContextManager" or "DistributedService" so you could get on with it and "stop wasting time thinking about names" (*BIG mistake!*). Unfortunately, neither of these nouns indicate any *particular* purpose *at all*, so this invited you (and/or your co-workers!) to add all kinds of irrelevant features. This problem is even worse (and probably more common too) when the compound noun has the name of a singular noun (when your DogVolcano is called just "Dog" even though it also expresses the Volcano concept). If you had taken the time to be clear about your naming you might have rejected your DogVolcano *before* you wrote all that buggy code!

Avoid mixing concepts.
Define a separate class for every unique concept,
using naming to guide the concept discovery process.

This is also one of the reasons, by the way, that most programmers have a terrible time with multiple-inheritance: when it's used wrongly, it can be used to create compound nouns. If you use multiple-inheritance of implementation, mixing two nouns together (DogVolcano extends Dog, Volcano) is a nightmare. Instead it's best to use secondary base classes as mix-ins or in terms of parts-of-speech, as *adjectives* (since they mix-in like properties to modify the meaning of the primary noun just as adjectives do in English). For example, FastBlueDog could be "class FastBlueDog extends Dog, Blue, Fast", which makes a lot more sense than a DogVolcano. Although Java does not allow this kind of mix-in, multiple inheritance of interfaces is very useful in Java and we will discuss that in the next chapter.

Another grammatical trap you can fall into is making poor decisions about which objects to use as "adjectives" (settable properties of an object which modify its nature) and which objects to use as "adverbs" (parameters to a method which modify only the action being performed). The difference between the two in this context is mainly that adverbs have more limited scope and don't change any object state (and less mutability is always better). So, when it is reasonable to do so it is better to pass parameters than set properties. For example, this:

```
RemoteResource resource = new RemoteResource(...);
resource.setRetrievalTimeout(Duration.seconds(30));
InputStream in = resource.download();
```

modifies object state and is not nearly as safe or readable as this:

```
InputStream in = new
RemoteResource(...).download(Duration.seconds(30));
```

Prefer well-abstracted parameters to properties.

Another common pitfall is to allow your code to become complex by letting related adverbs and adjectives proliferate (good writers cringe at sentences full of unnecessary adverbs and adjectives and Hemingway is probably rolling in his grave as we speak).

For example, you could add more parameters like a maximum size and a maximum access frequency to modify the behavior of the download verb:

```
InputStream in = new RemoteResource(...).download
  (Duration.seconds(30),
   Bytes.megabytes(30),
   Frequency.every(Duration.minutes(30)), ...);
```

But this all-too-common approach gets out of hand pretty quickly. Instead, consider if there is an abstraction possible by getting your thesaurus out to look for a more general adverb (in our world, these "adverbs" are technically nouns too, of course, since they are represented as objects, but they differ in that their *purpose* is adverbial since they modify the behavior of verbs such as download()).

With a better adverb as your abstraction, your code can be much easier to follow:

```
public class AccessConstraints
{
  Duration timeout;
  Bytes maximumSize;
  Frequency maximumAccessFrequency;

    [...]
}
```

This generalization, not only eliminates several parameters and allows your class to evolve without breaking clients, but it also helps to clarify your intention greatly. If you write this:

```
public class RemoteResource
{
  public InputStream download
    (Duration timeout, Bytes maximumSize,
     Frequency maximumAccessFrequency);
}
```

It takes more mental effort for your users to realize (if they do) that the parameters are all serving the same concept than if you write this:

```
public class RemoteResource
{
  public InputStream download
    (AccessConstraints constraints);
}
```

> *In the case of parameters in particular, less is more.*
> *Prefer fewer parameters and ensure that they are as*
> *conceptually all-encompassing as possible.*

Narrative

Once you have created a grammar that you can use to make statements about your domain, all that is left is to relate an interesting story using that grammar. While telling terse stories with "Domain Specific Languages" (DSLs) is all the rage right now, I think this should be taken with a grain of salt. It's far more important to create a clear and simple grammar that anyone can understand and to write a story that's easy to follow. If you create a good grammar, it will be highly expressive and compact, and you won't find yourself needing to repeat yourself. Which makes it less likely that a DSL would be of any use. In some sense, the grammar that a high quality object model forms *is* a "domain specific language" that just happens to have a common syntax (like Java).

Stories written with a rich, carefully constructed object model are extremely easy to read and edit. In fact, I can usually spot high quality object-oriented code from across a room, before I can even read the actual text. That's because good code has a certain shape. Typically, good OO code consists of a large number of simple, focused classes containing short, relatively self-explanatory methods. The overall appearance is one of bareness and simplicity.

Well-written code stories require relatively little in the way of documentation when compared with the terse, dense and unclear. Nevertheless, even in a well-written codebase, documentation serves several critical purposes. First, it is important at a high level to document the organization of packages and classes and their interrelationships. In Javadoc, this is done by creating package.html descriptors and is all too often ignored. Although it is important to explain in your package.html any non-obvious details about how your package works, the more important and long-lasting purpose in describing a package is to tell the story of what you were trying to accomplish. If the purpose of the package is clear, it will be clear to people refactoring code in your package how those changes can best serve your underlying purpose.

Second, methods that are not self-explanatory or which have non-obvious side-effects or threading concerns require Javadoc comments. It is actually a distraction to document completely uninteresting methods such as getters and setters (which, by the way, you should avoid creating in the first place, but that's a long story for another time) or methods whose function is obvious and unambiguous. It is also good practice to avoid boilerplate and to write sentences or grammatically correct phrases to describe method functionality and parameters. For example, "This method sets the duration value" is a completely useless comment and a waste of time for both coder and reader. More useful is a comment like "Finds the median salary of the given list of users. Although the median is found by sorting the list by salary, a copy of the list is made so that callers will not be affected." Most useful are critical comments like "Finds the median salary of the given list of users. Because this list can be extremely large it is sorted in place, which can affect callers or background threads which might access the list concurrently."

> *Strongly prefer meaningful comments that clearly relate*
> *intention and shed light on the non-obvious.*
> *Avoid boilerplate.*

Finally, any non-trivial code within a method requires single line comments. But even relatively simple code can benefit by enhancing readability and making intention clear. My suggestion here is to think of this documentation as a story-telling narrative whose purpose is to explain what you were trying to accomplish. I prefer to make the comments form sentences within the method. For example:

```
// If there is a list of listeners,
if (listeners != null)
{
  // make a copy of them
  List<Listener<Message>> copy =
    new ArrayList<Listener<Message>>(listeners);

  // sorted by priority,
  Collections.sort(copy, new PriorityComparator());

  // then loop through each listener,
  for (Listener<Message> listener : copy)
  {
    // dispatching the message to it.
    listener.onMessage(message);
  }
}
```

The running comment taken together then reads as an ordinary English sentence that describes the intention of the code (the story of what you were trying to do): "If there is a list of listeners, make a copy of them sorted by priority, then loop through each listener, dispatching the message to it." This is a fairly straightforward example, but the more complex the algorithm, the more important it will be to see the intention behind the code. Writing comments that tell a story

37

like this is very easy to read. It also works the other way around. When you can write the method's narrative, you can be more certain that your code is going to work.

> *Strongly prefer code and documentation which tell a simple,*
> *readable story of what your code is trying to do.*

Chapter 5

Modeling

"The map is not the territory" — *Alfred Korzybski*

When we create a program, we are always creating a simulation of something that happens (or which we believe happens) in the real world that we observe. Even an operation as fundamental as adding two integer values is, in reality, only a simulation. What we have done in *reality* is to create an electronic system in which we have decided to interpret certain patterns of electronic energy as "bits" of information, and the organization of these bits into particular relationships as designating numeric values. We then interpret a very particular process of rearranging bits automatically to be analogous to "adding." We don't often think about adding as a simulation because the simulation is so accurate that we accept it as "real." But as we create more complex programs, the gap between "the map" we are creating and "the territory" we are mapping becomes more apparent because the more complex a real-world process gets, the more complex it necessarily becomes to create a realistic simulation.

Coding is modeling. It is the act of mapping a real-world process (something we observe or believe to be true) onto a digital simulation of that process. The act of creating this map necessarily has two distinct phases: analysis and synthesis. First, we analyze the process we are trying to simulate and break it down into a set of concepts, relationships and behavior that we believe we understand. Then, we synthesize a digital model of those concepts, relationships and behavior.

The mark of the naive coder is that he does little or nothing to analyze and model the problem he wants to solve, instead focusing immediately on the instant gratification of *trying to get the code to do something*. The master craftsman, by contrast, ignores result and instead engages in a process of modeling the problem so accurately that making things happen becomes a second-order effect that is made almost inevitable by the structure of the model. In other words, the code will be set up so that the only thing it can do when it's all tied together is what was intended. Furthermore, the model will create a powerful and simple grammar for expressing many future thoughts in the domain being modeled. Code that is written like this is incredibly easy to debug and maintain, although you may not have experienced much code like this because, frankly, not that much of it exists in the software industry as a whole. It takes experience to get there, but even more importantly the kind of attention to process I'm attempting to convey in this book.

Avoid the temptation to get your code to do something.
Instead, focus on making your model clear and accurate.

Unfortunately, in any significant problem, both problem analysis and the creation of a simulation based on that analysis will necessarily introduce mapping errors. The problem will be insufficiently analyzed and the solution will inadequately express the analyzed system. While there is plenty of room to go wrong in synthesizing a solution, the worst errors are almost always those first-order conceptual errors where the real-world process has been inadequately investigated or simply misunderstood. The reason is simply that if you don't understand what it is you're trying to model, the best and most beautiful simulation in the world of that misunderstanding won't do any good. So what can we do? We can work to get better at analyzing and better at creating models. And again, we can work to understand and improve our own process for doing this.

Analysis

Julius Caesar was reputed to say "Divide et Impera" or "Divide and Conquer". He used this strategy to divide and conquer the Gauls, simplifying his war with them into a series of smaller conflicts, each more easily winnable on its own. This strategy of breaking down a larger problem into smaller, easier problems is really the *only* useful strategy I know of for addressing code complexity. This core strategy of divide and conquer actually takes on dozens if not hundreds of names in computer software. Here are just a few examples. At the large scale:

- The Internet itself divides and conquers the problem of routing information for the whole planet through a hierarchy of addressable sub-networks

- Enterprises divide and conquer problems of service quality and high availability by distributing data and service requests to network operations centers located in different geographical regions

- Enterprises divide and conquer large scale systems by using networks to organize servers into clusters and server farms

- Individual servers divide and conquer the problem of concurrent code execution by dividing code into processes

- Virtual machines divide and conquer the problem of varying run-time environments by dividing code description (byte code) from code implementation (machine code)

- Enterprise "tiers" divide and conquer large projects by organizing groups of related modules into independent service layers

- Modules divide and conquer the problem of organizing and configuring related sets of features

At the small scale:

- Packages divide and conquer code complexity and security issues by organizing related classes and resources

- Interfaces divide and conquer code binding issues by decoupling the intention to make a method call from the exact method to be executed

- Dependency injection and locator registries divide and conquer code binding location issues by decoupling the desire for an implementation from the source of the implementation

- Design patterns divide and conquer code complexity by decoupling the features of a design into smaller, simpler, more flexible classes

- Objects themselves divide and conquer through encapsulation by separating internal implementation from external use, yielding increased flexibility to change the implementation at a later date without affecting clients

I'm sure you can think of many, many more examples.

Getting back to our discussion of coding as modeling, it's quite reasonable to expect that any approach we might take to modeling a real world process is going to involve dividing it up into pieces. But the process that you use to analyze your problem and break it down will determine the quality of your model. And the quality of your model is the quality of your code.

Prefer expending effort on improving the quality of your model.
The model is everything.

You can find *some* dividing lines using a haphazard, even unconscious approach to analysis, whether it be experience, group consensus or gut instinct. But what separates the excellent, flexible, functional, testable and reusable from the ordinary is this:

The ability to find the clearest dividing lines that break a problem down fully.

The more detailed and precise your understanding of the concepts involved in the process you are trying to model, the more likely it is that you will identify ways to divide those concepts up cleanly. It takes time and practice to get really good at this, but you will find if you do practice mindfully that you get better and better at it.

Let's use a toy example to illustrate. Suppose we were trying to design a solution to a problem like "data validation". Instead of jumping to solutions by drawing UML or class diagrams (or, worse, writing code) it is more helpful to simply define the problem clearly first. This will then allow us to break that defined problem down into clean, non-overlapping concepts.

So, let's just start off with a vague, English definition of the problem of data validation:

Given an object, we want to be able to determine if it is in a valid state before we do something with it.

If we analyze this statement for a while, it raises quite a few questions. The most relevant ones I can think of right now are:

- What does valid mean?

- Who wants to know if the object is not valid?

- How do they want to be informed? By a returned value? By exception?

- What do they want to know?

- Do they want descriptions of all validity problems encountered or just valid/invalid?

- Are there different types of validity problems?

- Should problem descriptions be localized?

- How do we substitute constraint values into the descriptions?

- Can an object be partially valid?

- If the object validates itself (which is good OO design), there would be only one definition of valid. But don't we want to be able to validate an object in more than one way?

- Should the validity of the object include how that object's state relates to a larger scope or context? For example, in a form there might be an Address object and a PhoneNumber object and the form would be valid if the user provided either a valid address or a valid phone number.

> *State your problem. Then, ask every question*
> *you can think of before starting to design.*

There may be more questions, but let's suppose that if we've decided that if we had good answers to these questions that everyone would be pretty satisfied. Given that, we can investigate the questions in order to locate the base concepts that are involved. Each concept that we divide out is going to require its own micro-architecture and we will want to go through the whole process of modeling on each of those designs as well. If this sounds like a lot of work, by the way, consider what happens when you don't take this approach (as is overwhelmingly true today): in the worst case, you will actually wind up with N (completely untestable and non-interoperable) expressions of each of these micro-architectures inlined into any number of modules in any number of projects. At most companies, and even in most open source software, N is all too large a number. Rather than investigating and fully solving these basic, atomic problems, engineers routinely cut and paste or directly code solutions over and over. It's not hard to imagine all the effects this has on code quality.

> *Prefer micro-architecture to repeating common idioms.*
> *Strongly avoid cutting and pasting code!*

So after staring at these questions for a while, here are the basic concepts I have extracted, each in their most general form (and each deserving its own micro-architecture):

- Message - A micro-architecture for forming both internal messages and localized, user-facing messages would allow us to conveniently describe validation problems and warnings with arbitrary interpolated values such as validation constraints (maximum or minimum length, for example).

- Localizer - A micro-architecture for localizing messages would allow us to find text for messages in multiple languages.

- ResourceLocator - A micro-architecture for flexibly locating resources would allow us to find language resources for the Localizer.

- Locator - A micro-architecture for locating objects would allow us to locate resources for the ResourceLocator.

- VariableInterpolator - A micro-architecture for interpolating variables into strings would allow us to substitute values into a message.

- Listener - A micro-architecture for listening to messages would allow us to notify interested parties of validation issues. A MessageList Listener could build up a list of messages sent to it, allowing callers to iterate through the messages. A runtime-exception-throwing listener would allow callers to opt for exception throwing behavior instead.

- Broadcaster - A micro-architecture that supports the broadcaster design pattern would allow us to factor out sending validation problem notifications.

- Logger - A logging micro-architecture would ideally accept and log broadcasted messages, which would include problems broadcast by something that is Validatable.

- Validatable - Our validation micro-architecture should leverage all these pieces to create a highly extensible framework for doing validation in the abstract.

As you can see, once you have all these other micro-architectures co-operating together, the sum is greater than the parts and, most importantly, the Validatable micro-architecture is *only* about validation and not about any of the other concepts! By dividing our system into tight, simple, well-defined micro-architectures, we can create powerful synergistic effects. Our code under this design becomes:

- Simpler

- Smaller

- More focused

- More testable

- More reusable

> *Prioritize micro-architectural work over other work to the extent you can.*

Synthesis

Synthesis is the phase of process modeling where you begin to build up the micro-architectural simulation of the concepts that you extracted during analysis. There are a lot of issues to solve in each of these dependent architectures, but let's take a quick glance at what each top-level micro-architecture might look like in sketch form, and then use these terms to present a rough architecture for validation that should stand the test of time and reuse.

```
public interface Message
{
    String format();
}
```

A Message is an object that can be formatted into a String. You could also use Object's toString method and allow any object, but that's less explicit and would be prone to error (and, besides, it's easy enough to make an ObjectMessage wrapper which does a toString() for simple cases).

```
public class InterpolatedMessage implements Message
{
  public InterpolatedMessage(String message,
    Object... arguments);
  public String format()
  {
    [...]
  }
}
```

An InterpolatedMessage is just a message string with some arguments that can be formatted on demand. The actual implementation should do position-independent variable substitutions using a map of named values. This will allow for easy localization of messages.

```
public interface Listener<Message>
{
  void onReceive(Message message);
}
```

A Listener is just any object that can receive a message. Unfortunately, because Java's generics implementation does "type erasure", an object can currently implement only one Listener at a time!

```
public interface Broadcaster<Message>
{
  void broadcast(Message message);
}
```

A Broadcaster is some object that sends a message.

```
public interface Multicaster<Message>
  extends Broadcaster<Message>
{
  void addListener(Listener<Message> listener);
  void removeListener(Listener<Message> listener);
}
```

A Multicaster is a Broadcaster that allows you to add and remove listeners from a set. The listeners in this definition are unordered, but you can imagine implementations that allow the listeners to be ordered manually or even by specifying listener ordering constraints.

```
public interface Logger extends Listener<Message>
{
  void log(Message message);
}
```

A logger just listens to messages and logs them using its own log method.

Now that we have some of the other likely micro-architectures sketched out, let's start by defining what we think would be the minimum interface for validation and then see if we have what we need:

```
public interface Validatable<Problem>
{
  void validate(Listener<Problem> listener);
}
```

In this definition, a Validatable implements a validate() method that calls a problem listener when it encounters problems. This is a very atomic definition of validation. Some arbitrary piece of code does some checking on the object's fields and problems are broadcasted to the listener. Even the type of message that is sent to the listener is flexible. Since it is pretty hard to argue with this interface, let's accept this as a first cut and check it against the conceptual questions we came up with in the analysis section to see how we did.

- What does valid mean?

Valid means absolutely anything that a Validatable cares to implement. This is a good thing because we are not restricted. In fact, the Validatable interface we've come up with doesn't even specify what is to be validated, so it wouldn't prevent strange or unforeseeable use cases where multiple objects or contexts were involved.

- Who wants to know if the object is not valid?

- How do they want to be informed? By return value? By exception?

- What do they want to know?

- Do they want descriptions of all validity problems encountered or just valid/invalid?

Well, the listener wants to know if the object is not valid, of course. And since the listener can be any implementation whatsoever, Validatables are completely general. The listener can store messages in a list (which serves as a return value) or throw an exception, or just count the number of messages of a certain type. It's open.

- Are there different types of validity problems?

- Should problem descriptions be localized?

- How do we substitute constraint values into the descriptions?

We've decided on a Message base object, which will provide localization and variable interpolation, but this can be extended arbitrarily and it can serve as a base class for messages that get logged in the logging micro-architecture.

- Can an object be partially valid?

In our definition, actually, yes. Since different subclasses of Message might exist like Problem or Warning, the Validatable might send back one or more warnings, but no problems. It would then be up to the caller to determine if this was "valid enough." Note that this partial-success case is the reason I opted not to have validate return a boolean.

- If the object validates itself (which is good OO design), there would be only one definition of valid. But don't we want to be able to validate an object in more than one way?

With our interface, an object can implement Validatable itself, but there is nothing preventing some external Validator class implementing Validatable from taking that object as an argument in order to provide a second way to validate that object. So we get the best of both worlds.

- Should the validity of the object include how that object's state relates to a larger scope or context? For example, in a form there might be an Address object and a PhoneNumber object and the form would be valid if the user provided either a valid address or a valid phone number.

There is nothing in our design that makes this impossible. However, my instinct is that it would probably be best for the Form object itself to simply be Validatable.

A full implementation of our validation micro-architecture would probably include at least one base class to help us implement validators that are Validatable. This AbstractValidator would implement Validatable and could be used for convenience in objects to create in-place validators that implement Validatable.

```
public class MyObject implements Validatable
{
  [...]

  @Override
  public void validate(Listener<? extends Problem> lis-
tener)
  {
    new AbstractValidator()
    {
      protected void onValidate()
      {
        // do validation of MyObject
      }
    }.validate(listener);
  }
}
```

Building Practical Micro-Architectures

It will not always be practical to implement micro-architectures from the ground up. If there is a good one that serves your purposes *fully* (and you should think hard about this, not jump at immediate solutions, because you can create a lot of interoperability problems down the road by choosing poorly here), you should use that. But in the present state of the software world, more often than not, you will find yourself creating micro-architectures by wrapping other less-well-designed packages.

> *Prefer wrapping badly designed code in a quality micro-architecture to using it directly.*

I find myself doing this frequently with the JDK. Even Java collections can benefit from some augmentation, but one example of code particularly worth wrapping is Java's network package. This package is both poorly designed in object architecture terms AND highly incomplete in terms of my needs. Just thinking about the concepts involved for a minute will bring up a lot of missing conceptual territory. Just for starters, there is no Java object for a Host! And a port is not represented as a concept by any object either, but rather as a parameter to various procedural methods. And so on. The more you look, the more problems you will find. But if you break down Java networking the way we just did with validation and wrap it up in a better design and link it up to related micro-architectures, the result is pretty stunning (and unfortunately the proof of this won't fit in the margins here). Massive amounts of network access code disappears completely and code becomes truly object-oriented, self-describing, minimal, testable and reliable. The difference is like night and day. In fact it is so large that I would not recommend using Java's network functionality without a set of well-designed, micro-architectural wrappers. It takes time to do this work, but in the end you only do it once, as opposed to the usual route which is essentially to manually do the same work over and over and cross your fingers.

Improving Java

When James Gosling talks about Java he sometimes jokes that his biggest regret in designing the language was the inclusion of classes. When the laughter dies down, I think he's right. The problem with classes is that they don't provide strong enough decoupling and encapsulation guarantees. When you extend a class, you're tying your subclass to the implementation details of its superclass. In the worst-case, you can even have direct dependencies on fields in your superclass, but even dependencies on inherited methods are subject to change. Interfaces provide a better way to decouple objects so that their implementation details don't get intertwined. However, interfaces in Java at the present time are a pretty clumsy way to accomplish some of the effects that I desire. In this section, we take a look at some of the ways that the Java type system could possibly be improved to better enable micro-architecture.

Type Arithmetic

One problem regarding interfaces has to do with their "width". As we have seen in this chapter, narrower interfaces with fewer methods each having fewer parameters tend to have more power and generality. They have the potential to provide tightly defined, long-lasting conceptual definitions. Unfortunately, many interfaces today are too wide.

A first approach to solving this problem is to consider using multiple inheritance of interfaces to break down larger interfaces into finer conceptual surface areas, which can in turn be leveraged to permit the plugging of objects together that couldn't otherwise be fitted.

As an example of what I mean, the List interface in Java's collections package is a particularly "wide" interface. List itself has 25 methods and it extends the base Collection interface which has 15 more methods (for some reason, some of these methods overlap, but the point still stands that there are a lot of methods involved). This proliferation of methods limits the generality of code which wishes to work with just one of the concepts that List defines, which means that the client code using the List interface will be tied to the entire concept of 40 methods that define what it means to be a list.

Suppose instead, that we break List down into a set of micro-architectural sub-interfaces. Without defining all of them, a few of these might be:

```
public interface Indexable<Element>
{
  Element get(int index);
  void set(int index, Element object);
}

public interface Countable
{
  int count();
}
```

```
public interface Addable<Element>
{
  void add(Element object);
}
```

This raises many interesting questions about how to divide up the interface. For just one example, the Indexable interface here should probably be subdivided into a read and a write sub-interface because not all things that are indexed can be written to: the sequence of prime numbers is indexed, but the values are constant. But for the purposes of this discussion, you get the general idea.

At the present time in Java, you can combine two interfaces together only by explicitly defining a third interface that multiply inherits from both of those interfaces. What would be nice, and enable micro-architectures in general, would be some simple notion of "type arithmetic" which we could use to do things like combining interfaces on the fly.

Let's take a look at the Collections.sort(List) method as an example. Since sort() takes List as an argument, this means that any caller wanting to use Collections.sort() will have to implement the dozens of methods in the List interface contract. While this is made convenient by AbstractList, suppose you wanted to use some other collections library or you simply have your own custom data structure that is Indexable and Countable but not a List. One approach would be to use the Indexable and Countable "atoms" we broke out of the List interface to define a higher level "molecular" interface like this:

```
public interface Sortable<Element>
  extends Indexable<Element>, Countable
{
}
```

And this does work, but the problem with scaling this approach is that the Java language only allows explicitly declared interface combinations and there are simply too many combinations possible where a reasonably complex object is concerned (more on this below). Suppose instead that we could glue two interfaces together anywhere we wanted. We could then write a generalized sorting interface like this:

```
public interface Sorter<Element>
{
  void sort(Indexable<Element> + Countable elements);
}
```

The sort method in this interface now accepts our new conception of Lists, but it also will accept any type that is Countable and Indexable, which are the only two concepts from a list that are necessary to sort something. Now, with this micro-architectural approach, we can write a sorting implementation that will work with multiple collections libraries and custom data structures. We could even change the Java Array type so that it implements Countable and Indexable, which would make all arrays sortable by any Sorter. Finally, the Java language square bracket syntax could be generalized to work with *any* object that is both Indexable and Countable, which would include not only lists and arrays but any user-defined type whatsoever.

Some astute, advanced readers may have realized already that type arithmetic like this is possible today, and technically they are correct, as the generics "&" operator can be used to combine types. That said, there are at least a couple of drawbacks. One simple one is that due to type erasure, overloaded methods with different type combinations would clash. Another much uglier problem is that it would be awkward at best to declare many different fields and local variables simultaneously with combined types using generics. Finally, the resulting code (below) is more verbose and hard to read than it could be for something that should be a common, everyday practice which is easily and intuitively understood by beginners. However, if you are adventuresome and want to try "type arithmetic" with generics today, you can write Sorter like this:

```
public interface Sorter<Element>
{
  <Sortable extends Indexable<Element> & Countable>
    void sort(Sortable elements);
}
```

You may be thinking that there are still other alternate ways to handle type combining, but with enough conceptual complexity, language support for "type arithmetic" starts to look like a compelling idea.

Thinking about micro-architecture reminds me of an interesting conversation I had many years ago when I was working on the Swing team at Sun Microsystems back in the early days of Java. Some people on the team were of the opinion that Component should be an interface and others that it was best as an abstract class. But really, neither sounded like a good choice. Abstract class is an unfortunate choice because it makes mock-object testing hard and limits Swing to one implementation of Component. But Component would be very awkward as a single interface as well, because it includes a large and growing collection of concepts. If component were an interface, every time you wanted to add a new feature to Component, you would break every piece of code that depended on that interface. While you can work around this by defining Component2, Component3 and so on, it seemed like there must be a better way.

The root problem, as I see it, is that Component and List (and many other Java classes) are not micro-architectural. The fact that they are molecules that are not composed of smaller atomic concepts limits reuse and causes interoperability problems. It would be more ideal if Component were an abstract class that implemented many narrow interfaces, one for each capability that the Component supports:

```
public abstract class Component implements Sizable,
   Locatable, Drawable, Visible, Enabled, Parented,
   BackgroundColored, Focusable, Named, Clickable, [...]
{
   [...]
}

public interface Sizable
{
   void setSize(Dimension dimension);
}

public interface Locatable
{
   void setLocation(Point point);
}

public interface Drawable
{
   void repaint();
}
```

Now, if we wanted to make a class that could animate Components by moving them around, we could do that by binding only to the relevant concepts that Component exposes. This would allow us to write very general animation algorithms. For example, we could define an animator that "minimizes" a Component, shrinking it from its current size down to zero size at the origin over a period of time. But this minimizer would work with not only Components, but actually any object that is Sizable, Locatable and Drawable. It becomes easy and clean to unit test our Minimizer with a mock object. And since it's not coupled to the concept of "Component", it could be used to animate non-component objects like, for example, a game sprite being drawn on an off-screen buffer. We have fully decoupled "minimizing" from Component, making the resulting class fully reusable.

```
public interface Minimizer
{
  void minimize(Sizable + Locatable + Drawable
    minimizable, Duration duration);
}
```

If you're wondering at this point if I am suggesting that Java itself should define micro-architectural interfaces, I am. In fact, although I support Java closures too, the best way to move forward in
terms of software quality, reusability and interoperability is not to
make it easier to write terse software, but to very carefully enable better and cleaner ways to combine objects within the language itself. *It's
not that we cannot write enough software today (clearly we can!) it's that the software we write doesn't play nicely together.*

Type Enhancers

Another potential way to improve encapsulation and reuse in
Java is to provide a different "type arithmetic" mechanism for "mixing in" functionality that I call a "type enhancer". The twist here is to
allow the mixing of types as in multiple inheritance, but to do it
through public interfaces, without mixing any implementation details. A type enhancer uses a "that" reference passed to its constructor
to talk to the type that it is enhancing through the enhanced type's
public interface. Because only the public interface is used, you can
even enhance a final class like String:

```
public enhancer BeanStyle
{
  private String that;

  public BeanStyle(String that)
  {
    this.that = that;
  }
```

```
public String toCamelCase()
{
  StringBuilder builder = new StringBuilder();

  // Append camel-cased version of "that" to builder

  return builder.toString();
}
}
```

The enhancer would then be used like this:

```
public void myMethod()
{
  BeanStyle + String value = "test";
  value.toLowerCase();
  value.toCamelCase();
}
```

Or if many uses of a given enhanced type were desired, a simple arithmetic syntax could be defined, declaring a lasting combination:

```
public class BeanString = String + BeanStyle;

class MyClass
{
  void myMethod()
  {
    BeanString value = "test";
    value.toLowerCase();
    value.toCamelCase();
  }
}
```

This would provide a potential solution for new Java coders who want to enhance String but soon discover that String cannot be extended. It would also enable much more powerful and more microarchitectural design in general.

Type Binding

Finally, Java could be improved through some kind of linguistic parallel to the new operator which does type binding. The new operator is an incredibly natural way to create objects and I leveraged that in creating the Wicket framework to great effect. People like "new". In fact, using it is so natural that I often prefer using the new operator and a very simple interface locator micro-architecture to dependency injection even though I *do* understand some of the benefits of dependency injection.

I think what we need in java is a new operator for type binding. Or more likely two operators: "bind" and "provide". Bind should declare the need for an interface of a specific type whose implementation can be located within the enumeration of all available objects declared by "provide" statements for the same interface. Specific implementations could be located by some simple extension of Java's enum concept. The JVM then would do the binding at runtime and Spring and Google Guice could be retired.

Improving Software Industry Process

Reflecting on the generally miserable state of code quality in the software industry, I think more focus on process and writing clear, reusable software would open up a lot of doors that are presently unavailable. It would be a good idea, for example, for every large company to have a dedicated, full-time software reuse group. But even mid-sized companies and smart, forward-thinking companies of smaller sizes may wish to consider this possibility as well. With some commitment and creative thinking, reasonable models for improving software process and code quality can be created even at the very smallest organizations. For example, instead of hiring an entire team to solve process and reuse problems, a more resource-constrained company could allocate as little as a single developer with sharp, object-oriented design skills, or even just part of that person's time.

> *Prefer software reuse and consider it an important product quality issue.*

Once a foothold has been established by creating some kind of *formal focus* on the refinement of software process, it is relatively easy to iterate on that and expand what has been started. One interesting idea here is this: software product groups (particularly those that are experiencing quality issues) might send a team member to a "software process and code reuse group" (hereafter "process group") for a "tour of duty." On this tour of duty, they could learn new techniques, exchange ideas and work on their individual and group software process skills under the guidance of an expert while they work together to design practical reusable software that can be applied to their group's problems when they return to their group at the end of their tour of duty.

People with problems and a desire to improve their software process come in and people with new solutions and new skills and increased awareness of process come out. For junior level engineers this forms a sort of "software process and reusability boot camp" while for senior people it is a place to sharpen OO design skills and process. It may even be useful once a process group has been running a while to simply initiate *all* new developers at a company by sending them on a tour of duty so that they will understand the company's software process methodologies (not to mention getting educated on available reusable code) which can enable them to create high quality software from the very start.

While creating an environment that practices software quality does require leadership (senior-level OO skill and experience and the ability to communicate that), there could be a tendency towards building "ivory tower" software architecture (something divorced from practical application). The best idea to prevent a cultural gap here is to simply ensure that everyone at the company gets a chance to play on a regular basis and discover over time their own best way of creating software. Rotating practicing software engineers through a process group has the potential to effectively bridge that gap between practice and theory that Yogi Berra was referring to in the quote at the top of Chapter 3 ("In theory there is no difference between theory and practice. In practice there is.")

It is important to note that participants in a process group of this sort would receive not only technical mentoring from the group leader(s) but also participate in process discussion and mentoring. This meta-analysis is even more critical than the technical skills or the reusable software components, because engineers need to be able to not only solve software quality problems themselves but bring reliable process to bear on analyzing *the processes which created them in the first place.* Through this approach, ideally, an entire organization can iteratively teach itself its own best software processes.

An important side effect of creating a cycle of iterative discovery, improvement and practical application is that it has the potential to boost morale. Even bad, buggy legacy software can be fixed over time by expanding out small pockets of competence. By creating an engine that will drive these pockets of competence outwards throughout the entire organization, and by giving engineers the facilities to discover their own best engineering process, the company can become an *enabler* to its software designers, who already want to move in the direction of creating artful code that serves business needs. In my experience, even the promise that things *will be improving* because a new direction has been set can be enough to re-energize an unenthusiastic group or even a whole company.

Chapter 6

Faith

"He conquers who endures." — *Persius*

Most of us work in production environments that test our faith in our own coding process on a daily basis. Unfortunately, the first reaction we have when something goes wrong is to doubt ourselves rather than relying on the process we have been refining. It's all very easy to say "slow down to hurry up" or "don't prematurely optimize your code." It is much more difficult in practice to observe these maxims and stick to your guns when the going gets tough. So I want to take this opportunity to encourage you to instill some faith in yourself and to observe what happens when you are faithful to your process and what happens when you fail to observe your process under pressure.

Trust Objects

If you're coding in Java, you're coding in a language that has tremendous power to express powerful, compact solutions in object-oriented terms. It can also be used to express verbose, unreliable solutions that are really nothing more than procedural programming at its worst. The difference between solutions in the first category and solutions in the second category is generally experience plus faith.

When an experienced programmer trusts that they should create a tightly focused object for every concept and not skip steps in building their model, good things virtually always happen. And in the odd case where the first result is not ideal, their well-structured code permits easy optimization. When programmers of all levels of experience stop trusting that they should create the best structure first and optimize later, a mess inevitably results. *Do not prematurely optimize.* And in today's world of cheap, powerful, multicore server class machines and highly optimized VMs, this advice goes doubly (it is, by the way, *extremely cheap* to allocate objects in Java now — far cheaper than a traditional heap allocation). *Do not prematurely optimize.* You've heard it before and you will hear it again. It's a maxim because it is true from countless experiences, and it applies not only to performance but to all aspects of modeling. If you create the clearest, simplest model without worrying about the proliferation of classes, you will get the best results. And if performance ever does become an issue (which it often doesn't), you will have created the best structure to tune.

Strongly prefer delaying all forms of optimization.

When I talked with Eelco Hillenius (a friend and committer on the Apache Wicket project) about this book, his first thought was that if you're going to lean in one direction or the other, it is better to "over-engineer" a project than to "under-engineer" it. It's incredibly difficult to do anything with non-object-oriented code. By it's very nature it lacks the very most fundamental divide-and-conquer technique that there is: objects. If you keep your faith in objects and worry less about "over-engineering", you will find yourself rewarded.

Especially on today's server class machines, I find myself with the luxury to expand out my faith in objects more and more. If you look at almost any primitive type value, you can probably find reasons to make it either a domain object or a reusable object. When I created the micro-architecture for Countable above, I very nearly changed the code to:

```
public interface Countable
{
    Count count();
}
```

After all, isn't count a pretty fundamental concept in coding? It seems arguable that a count is not really best represented by a Java "int" primitive value, because negative counts are invalid. If we had a Count object instead, we could check these count primitive values whenever Count objects were constructed and throw an appropriate exception, allowing us to catch potential errors early. I can think of a number of other reasons why count deserves its own class as well (I'm not saying, by the way, that I'd make this design decision for an interface as broad as Countable — at least not without rewriting most of the Java core libraries as well). For one thing, Count is more type-safe than int. For another the Count class itself makes code involving counts self-documenting. But maybe even more importantly, we can expand the Count implementation to include new features. For example, It might also be nice to have toString() return a more human-readable, comma-separated string representation for larger values. A Count object could even implement the Iterable interface so you could plug it into an advanced for loop. But whether you agree or not (and there are a lot of unanswered questions here!), it's good food for thought. And again, when in doubt, always build your faith.

> *Prefer creating more (simple, focused) classes using*
> *the processes described in this book.*
> *It may feel awkward at first, but that's normal.*
> *It takes time to create new habits.*

Trust Your Team

Besides communicating well with the Java virtual machine, you need to spend lots of time communicating with your team so that you can build the same kind of process trust with them that you're building with yourself in your own craft. It is important to have the sort of discussions described in Chapter 2 so that you can establish a powerful group dynamic. But another part of establishing a strong group dynamic is to reinforce trust in your coding process in each other.

When deadlines approach and faith gets weak, one of my strengths as a leader is to remind people on my team that they need to slow down to hurry up and that they should trust their process. My experience is helpful here because I am a believer: maintaining faith in object-oriented design process inevitably gets you where you need to go not only better but also faster. If you've stuck with your process and built a well-structured codebase, why give up on it at the last minute?

Work to reinforce faith in your group's process.

Trust Yourself

Finally, you need to trust yourself. It will take time, but the process that you're building by bringing awareness and thoughtful focus to your work life will pay off. If you haven't experienced it for yourself, take it from someone who's been there and done that.

So go forth and do the work! Over time I have faith that you will transform your ordinary coding work into an incremental, artful process that is constantly growing and improving.

Enjoy!

www.ingramcontent.com/pod-product-compliance
Lightning Source LLC
Chambersburg PA
CBHW061031050326
40689CB00012B/2771